MarketAtomy

What to Expect
When Expecting a Business

MarketAtomy

What to Expect
When Expecting a Business

Danna J. Olivo

YouSpeakIt
PUBLISHING
The Easy Way
to Get Your Book
Done Right™

www.YouSpeakItPublishing.com

ISBN: 978-1-945446-18-4

Dedication

To my husband, David, who has believed in me from the beginning and trusted in me to get where I needed.

Te amo con todo mi corazón.

Acknowledgments

I have encountered many amazing individuals during this journey of self-growth and enlightenment. Life happens because of the relationships we encounter throughout the journey. I would like to acknowledge my family and friends who have contributed to this process along the way.

Thank you to my husband, David, first and foremost. Thank you for encouraging me to keep moving forward with my dream, by starting the funding for my first book, *Success from the Heart*. Thank you for the love, protection, and strength you bring as a husband, friend, and confidant.

Thank you to those who helped me during the long physical and emotional healing process after my accident, especially my children, Stephanie and Bryce; and all four of my sisters, Debbie, Stacy, Renee, and Dawn, whose continuous support encourages even when we agree to disagree. Love is strengthened through adversity.

Thank you to Stacy, who took care of me after every one of my surgeries, and to my life coach, Marty Ward, who helped me get to the root of my PTSD and my fear of getting back out in the world and back to work.

To my orthopedic physician, Dr. Michael Riggenbach, who never gave up, even when I didn't think I could go through another surgery, and finally, to my best friend and constant source of encouragement, Cathy Rodriguez. Love you all.

Also, thank you to Keith, Maura, and the Team at YouSpeakIt Publishing. Without their guidance and support, this book would still be an unrealized dream. I'm grateful for their assistance to make this book a reality.

Preface

When Danna first explained the MarketAtomy concept, I got it.

Now, that might not seem like a big deal, but working as an engineer all my life, I'm used to working with math and science, so marketing seemed like magic to me.

When she compared a business to a human body, pointing out that for each we need a strategy, I could see the connection. If you want to keep your body fit, healthy, energetic, and pain free, you need to have a strategy. This strategy impacts all the decisions you make in your life — what you eat, drink, how much you exercise, how much you sleep, what you do for leisure, and so on.

If you don't even think about any of these things, well, that too is a strategy. By not paying attention to any of these things, but doing only what feels good, you'll wind up with a body based on not paying attention. Depending on your actions this could be good or bad.

In business you also need a strategy and all your business decisions should to be based on that strategy. Once you are clear on the basics — such as *who* is your customer, *where* do you find them, *what* do you want to do for them — only then can you develop a strategy to go out and get your customers. Most of us in business don't have infinite money, so we can't operate like big companies. We must invest our money wisely and pursue marketing that yields measurable results.

What we as strategists often see, however, is that many new and seasoned entrepreneurs lack a clearly defined strategy at the start. They begin implementing solutions that don't quite fit. It's as if you took pieces out of different puzzle boxes, because you like the picture. In the end, you might have really cool individual pictures, but they won't fit together to create single whole picture because you didn't start with the end in mind.

A business-growth strategy begins with the end in mind, so all your decisions compliment your strategy to ultimately end up where you want to go.

If you have pain in your foot, would you go to the eye doctor because they are having a $39 special? Of course not; yet in business, people purchase solutions, because it's such a deal, because there was a webinar special, or — God forbid — it was FREE, rather than first consider: *does it support my strategy?*

That is the MarketAtomy concept in the words of an engineer, a non-marketer. Similar to a human body, everything needs to be working together. As you know, just a simple ingrown toenail can throw you out of whack!

David Olivo

VISION Engineer for MarketAtomy

Contents

Introduction   13

CHAPTER ONE
Your Closet Entrepreneur   19
   We All Have A Passion
      That We Want To Share   19
   We're All Experts At Something   23
   Turning Your Passion And Conviction
      Into A Business   27

CHAPTER TWO
A Heart To Help Others   33
   Teaching Others Through Your Stories
      And Lessons Learned   33
   Gaining Strength Through Vulnerability   39
   Leaving A Legacy   46

CHAPTER THREE
The Fears That Hold Us Back   53
   The Root Of All Your Obstacles Are Your
      Fears   53
   Confront Your Fears To Get Past Them   61
   Enlightenment   69

CHAPTER FOUR

The Marketatomy Concept Expanded   79

Marketing And Branding
Are The Heart Of Any Business   79

The Brain Holds The Playbook
For Your Business   86

The Heart And The Brain
Work In Tandem   91

CHAPTER FIVE

Realizing Your Dreams   99

Your Dreams Are Achievable   99

Your Dreams Are Your Own   106

Know Where You're Going,
So You'll Know When You Get There   112

Conclusion   119

Next Steps   123

About the Author   125

Introduction

MarketAtomy was conceived during a period of personal transformation following my near-death experience in 2012. Interestingly enough, the original idea began to take shape in the early 2000s, but the true impact did not fully take root until early 2013.

MarketAtomy is about understanding how to successfully take the dream of entrepreneurship from the gestational or concept stage, through the birth stage, and finally, through the growth stage. Within these pages I share lessons learned as a result of two failed businesses and years of strategic consulting experience with early stage companies. I'll teach you what needs to be put in place so that you can make intelligent decisions on how to set up your business model and position it for growth, and those you'll need in your circle to help you along the way.

I wrote this book because entrepreneurship is something that has been ingrained in my heart for many years. The number of failed small businesses across the United States is costing billions of dollars as new entrepreneurs invest their hard-earned savings — the equity that they have built over their lifetimes — to invest in something that's often destined to fail.

Why?

The majority of new businesses are launched with a good product or service, but without the skill level and knowledge base needed to successfully run the actual business. This is where my heart is: I see this happening and it just kills me. I want to reduce the number of failed businesses. I hope to do this by equipping you with the tools and education needed to succeed. I don't want you to end up losing your life savings, your retirement, or your home because you have invested in a company in which the odds for success are stacked against you from the get-go.

As you read these pages, reflect on your original dream. Remember what motivated you to go into business for yourself.

What is driving this dream of entrepreneurship?

As you read the book, think about how you would raise a child. You go through the process of planning, setting up your finances, doing everything that needs to be done when this child enters the world. The strategic process for creating your own business is the same. That is the gestational period: those things that need to be done before you open your business.

Then, after the birth of your child:

- You have to care for them.
- You have to teach them.
- You plan for their growth until they are self-sustaining.

That's exactly what you're going to do with your business, as well.

You open the business, and you need to grow it by:

- Attracting more customers
- Branding your business
- Putting yourself in the marketplace

Just as you send your child to school so that they can learn how to sustain themselves once they're adults, you will need to learn how to be an effective business owner.

New business owners need to learn that this is a *process*. It is not going to happen overnight. It takes patience and understanding that there will be stumbling blocks. You will run up against fears, just like you do when raising children. You fear for their safety. You fear for them making mistakes, and you want to be there to protect them.

You're going to do the same thing with your business, and get it to the point where it will sustain itself or you decide to sell it, so that you can move to the next stage in your life. This is very much like a child moving out or getting married.

You will gain an understanding of the processes that must be put in place to succeed in business, as well as an understanding of the motivation and forward momentum needed to keep that business growing to reach your goals. You'll also want to have an end goal in mind. Just like raising children, ultimately you want them to become self-sufficient adults, so that they can go off and start their own lives and families. You want to do the same with your business. You want to grow it to the point where it's self-sustaining, you can pass it on to the next generation, or you can sell it.

There are many resources available to help you. Rather than trying to do it on your own, use these resources, whether through the MarketAtomy learning platform at www.MarketAtomy.com, the Small Business Administration (SBA), its free mentoring services (SCORE), or anywhere else. Seek the help you need. Don't be afraid to ask for help from those who've been in your shoes.

CHAPTER ONE

Your Closet Entrepreneur

WE ALL HAVE A PASSION THAT WE WANT TO SHARE

I believe there's an entrepreneur in each of us. We are all good at *something*, but we may not think that it's something we can use as a business concept. A stay-at-home mom, for example, might be great at raising kids or managing a lifestyle, but she may not think those skills can translate into a business. We can all learn from each other's life experiences. Everyone has an entrepreneurial spirit inside them. The goal is identifying where that entrepreneur lies, and how to build or manifest upon your skills and talents and turn it into revenue on the back end.

Life and Work Experiences

I have more than forty years' experience working in marketing, branding, business development, sales, and strategic planning. Throughout those forty years, I have learned many lessons that offer great value for new entrepreneurs just starting out.

One of the lessons I've learned is the need for systems and processes. This is the strategic side of a business. Housewife, student, lawyer, or dockworker — whatever your current occupation — these systems are what you develop to make your job easier. These systems and processes have value.

As far as systems and processes, what also adds to the value that life and work experiences bring to the table are the relationships you've established.

In your job and career environments, you've built many relationships, many of which impact:

- The way you think
- The way you work
- The way you interact with others
- The way you manage and motivate others to do what you want them to do

All of these systems, processes, and relationships play a key role in entrepreneurship.

Life Stories

Your stories — the major events that have happened in your life — add validity to your entrepreneurial efforts. I can look back on my life and see many major events that have affected my future. As a result, with every one of these events, I have had to take a step back, reevaluate, and grow from that experience.

The story that brings with it lessons learned and the MarketAtomy concept, is that in 2012, I was working in Brazil as an independent representative for several U.S. firms when I was hit by one of Brazil's rapid buses as I was crossing the street to my apartment. After this unfortunate incident, I spent two months in Brazil recuperating before I could even fly home—and this put my business on hold for almost six months.

My thoughts from that time—my stories—and the lessons I learned, included:

- How I coped with all that surrounded my accident in a country whose language I did not speak well

- How being hit by a bus affected my business

Foremost in my mind was how I was going to ease my husband's fears when he finally got to Brazil and saw the condition I was in.

I used tools to communicate with my caregiver while I was recuperating. We used Google Translate to be able to communicate with each other. When you're up against the wall and have limited resources, you will be amazed by how creative you can be.

Understanding that I was in Brazil on business—and that business does not necessarily stop—I found myself entertaining clients at my apartment while I was recuperating. I also had a good team of representatives in Brazil who stepped up to the plate to keep things moving forward. However, because I was the primary point of contact for my business in Brazil, I took a pretty big financial hit as a result of the accident.

This is a good example of how you can use your stories to:

- Help grow your business
- Demonstrate transparency
- Build credibility

Frustrations — Product

Here's a funny story.

When we see a silly or simple product advertised on a shopping network or in an infomercial, many of us think: *Wow! That is such a simple product! Why didn't I think of that?*

Or you may have thought: *I had that idea, but I never did anything with it.*

Recently a girlfriend and I were talking about our eyebrows and how we have to color them to cover up the grey, now that we're getting up in age.

We said, "There's no product out there that will allow us to do this without having to go to a salon."

As we continued to discuss this, we decided to do some research to see if that was true — did anyone offer eyebrow dye?

We even came up with a name for our product: *Brow Wow*. As we got further into our research we found that there were several products on the market already, so the idea didn't take root. Taking steps like these, however, is how businesses get started.

Think of the Pet Rock that appeared on the market in the mid-1970s. It was just something that was simple and silly, but people were spending money to buy these rocks! There were even accessories for the Pet Rocks that could be bought as an up-sell.

There's always something to build a business around.

Don't dismiss your ideas. You need to look at them for what they are. They are good ideas that you have learned from, and others can benefit from what you've already learned.

WE'RE ALL EXPERTS AT SOMETHING

I encourage you to find your unique expertise because we're all human beings trying to find the most feasible, economic, and easiest way of doing things. We all learn through our life experiences. The lessons you've learned will go a long way in possibly helping your next-door neighbor, a friend, colleague, or family member.

A Lifetime of Lessons Learned

Lessons come in all forms, and can come into play at just the right time for someone down the road. An example of this involves my best friend and her husband. It's their second marriage, and they have a teenage daughter who was giving them a lot of trouble. They were frustrated because they couldn't seem to get through to her. My husband and I raised our daughter through her teen years and she is now a healthy, happy mother of three. We were able to pass on the lessons we learned in raising our daughter to help them with their daughter.

We were able to provide encouragement and reassure them that there is a bright light on the other side.

This happens in business as well as in our personal lives. We struggle, and we hope to learn from the mistakes we've made. We can help others through their struggles because of our experiences going through the same hardships and ultimately coming out the other side.

We've Developed Processes That Make Our Lives Easier

As I indicated earlier in the story about working within the industry and developing systems and processes, many times you may find yourself in a fight-or-flight mentality. You either dig in your heels and make it work, or you retreat and run away. You're thrown into an uncomfortable situation, and as a result you develop systems that will help you more easily manage that situation or event. Having learned from this, you can offer your stories, lessons, and expertise to the benefit of others.

For example, a major construction management company hired me in 2006. At the time that I was hired, I considered it an advancement in my career and another stepping stone toward where I wanted to be. I didn't realize when I took the position that they had absolutely no systems in place. This was a major international organization with hundreds of offices through the nation and the world.

As the result of that lack of systems, it took me four times as long to do a simple task because I was constantly chasing down information. The first six months that were required of me in my new position were spent simply putting systems in place just to make my job easier. That took a lot of time, but once I was able to get those systems in place, the time it took to complete those processes was cut by 75 percent.

Making Others' Lives Easier

At this construction management company, once I had the right systems in place, it was easier to teach other colleagues to follow those processes, which helped streamline the entire delivery process. In addition, I am sure—but I can't back this up, because I was laid off during the economic recession—that the systems I'd put in place made the transition easier for whomever they hired in my place.

It's always important to understand that these processes are constantly changing as you continue to grow and learn, as well. Remember that there are many means to an end. Someone always has a way to build a better mousetrap, as they say.

Don't minimize what you know or you've learned. It always has value to somebody else who may not have been through what you've experienced.

TURNING YOUR PASSION AND CONVICTION INTO A BUSINESS

Any business you start has to be driven by passion. Passion underlies everything. That passion has to reside in your gut. You need to believe strongly enough in it and its ability to bring in revenue and growth to someone else.

Ideas That We Should've, Could've — The Pet Rock Theory

MarketAtomy was developed because of a gap I saw in the market among new entrepreneurs. I saw an issue in which individuals — new entrepreneurs — were going into business without having any business knowledge. This was especially prevalent right after our most recent recession. Many new entrepreneurs jumped onto the entrepreneurship bandwagon simply because they could not find work and needed to bring in a paycheck. They had a quality product or service, but they didn't know how to run a business or bring customers through the door.

My passion was that I hated to see these people wasting their money running a business when they did not have the knowledge base to make it successful. During the process of working with these new entrepreneurs, I developed MarketAtomy. It originally began as a visual representation to illustrate what needed to be in place to successfully grow their businesses. By drawing that visual, and explaining it graphically, I could show entrepreneurs where their product or service fit into their overall business, and what needed to be in place around it to attract customers.

Passion and Conviction Drive the Business — Without It, the Business Fails

As I indicated earlier, passion is the underlying aspect to any successful business. If you don't believe in what you're doing, you can't sell it. If you can't sell it, you're not going to be able to bring customers through the door. The fact of the matter remains: without customers, there is no business.

Two of the main reasons for going into business are to serve and to create revenue. To create revenue, you need customers. In order for those customers to come through your door, they have to be made aware of your product or service. They have to understand what the product is and how it benefits them. They have to know about the product, and they have to be sold on the benefits and features of that product or service. Your passion is what drives that. Your passion creates the energy that draws the customer to you.

Your Passion Attracts Customers

Again, your passion is the energy you put into the universe. That passion, or energy, is what attracts potential customers to you. As they see you, and they see the energy that is generated, they're attracted to you. They want to learn more.

MarketAtomy, as I stated, is a graphic illustration of the makeup of a successful business. Because of the passion I have behind it, MarketAtomy has evolved into an online learning platform for entrepreneurs to gain the knowledge base they need to grow their businesses. This is where my passion drives the need or the desire, and as a result, the solution is provided.

If you don't have passion or conviction and the ability to communicate your passion, there's no way that you are going to attract customers to your business. They're not going to trust you. They're not going to see your commitment to your product or service and your ability to meet their need. They're not going to want to spend their hard-earned dollars on your product or service if you don't believe in it.

Call to Action!

One tool we use to help assess your passion
is the *Strengths, Weaknesses, Opportunities, and
Threats* (SWOT) Analysis. Although this tool is
generally used as a strategic tool for positioning,
we have also found it useful in homing in on your
passion. Typically your passion will lie within
your strengths. By identifying your strengths you
find your passion. A complimentary template is
available for you at www.marketatomy.com/
bktools.

CHAPTER TWO

A Heart to Help Others

TEACHING OTHERS THROUGH YOUR STORIES AND LESSONS LEARNED

When the original idea for MarketAtomy came to me, I reflected on my early childhood and adolescence, moving into adulthood. The bulk of my learning and growth was gained through school, taught by my parents, my teachers, and mentors. However, I realized that the lessons that really stuck with me were the ones that altered the course of my life. They're the ones in which I learned through my mistakes.

I was never the type of child who learned simply by listening to others. I had to experience it and make my own decisions. Sometimes this worked out well for me, sometimes not so much.

What I learned through all of my life lessons — good and bad — is what has shaped me into the person I am today: someone who does not rest on her laurels, but rather is constantly seeking to build a better mousetrap. I encounter a problem, and I seek a solution. This is the mindset of a true entrepreneur.

You Build Credibility

What really stuck with me through my mistakes and the lessons I've learned over the years were the impact that these lessons had on building my character. They helped to solidify me as an expert. With these lessons, I can now go into the world, talk to others about my experiences, and teach them what I have learned. It doesn't just apply to the business side; it applies to the personal side as well.

I have learned many lessons both personally and professionally. One example on the personal side I mentioned in Chapter One, raising my teenage daughter. She's now thirty-six, and what I'm about to describe happened back when she was a typical teenager — thirteen, fourteen, or fifteen. I know we all have our own stories about raising difficult teens, so I won't begin to think that I'm the only one to raise a difficult child and come out on the other side. As I said, this very intimate experience with my daughter helped me mentor my best friend when she was going through a similar situation with her teenage daughter. My husband and I were able to be there for her and her husband as a support system as they were going through their teenager's drama. We were able to guide them and support them as they were going through this same situation.

On the business side, two failed businesses have equipped me with a knowledge base of what *not* to do and what to watch out for when it comes to helping other new entrepreneurs. For example, I had those two failed businesses under my belt before I went back to school and received my degrees in Business, Marketing, and Management Information Systems (MIS). I realized after the fact that the reason these businesses failed was that I did not know what the hell I was doing. Therefore, I made incorrect and costly decisions that ultimately led to the demise of my businesses. These lessons are what drive my purpose behind MarketAtomy, which is all about preparing new entrepreneurs to succeed and, I hope, reduce the number of failed new businesses in the United States and ultimately around the globe.

Show Vulnerability

One thing I have struggled with through my entire life is vulnerability. Being the oldest of seven children, there were many times when I felt I was just a cog in a wheel, a means to an end. I very seldom felt as though I had a purpose or a place in my family environment. Because of that, I sought ways to elevate myself, to stand out and gain the recognition I so desperately wanted as a child. I immersed myself in activities where I could express my innermost feelings, such as art and writing. As you can imagine, I learned very early on how to self-motivate, as well as how to hide my vulnerabilities from the outside world.

Later on, I learned that as a female professional in a highly male-dominated industry — the architectural engineering and construction market — vulnerability equated weakness. I felt that I constantly had to prove my abilities to move forward in my career and gain the respect I deserved. As a result, my drive for success was often looked on as a negative characteristic among my colleagues. I had a goal, and I was going to achieve that goal, come hell or high water.

What I realized, well into my career, was that without my BS degree, there was an invisible glass ceiling that would not allow me to move up. It was then that I swallowed my pride and accepted the fact that I needed to go back to school and earn my degree. For the first time in almost twenty-five years, I stepped out of the corporate world and sent myself back to school. If anyone thinks that working at a job is harder than going back to college, I challenge them. Getting my degree was the hardest job I ever held in my life.

Probably my most recent lesson in vulnerability involved my recuperation from the very serious accident in 2012 in Rio de Janeiro, Brazil. I was working as an international consultant for several companies from the United States that wanted to break into the

Brazilian market. I happened to be crossing the street to my apartment after a long, hard day of meetings, and that's when I was hit by a bus that was traveling about forty-five miles an hour.

The end result was almost two months recuperating in a country where, as I mentioned, my understanding of the culture and the language were extremely limited, at best. I had representatives in the country willing to help me in any way possible, but putting myself completely in their hands was a difficult process for me.

I had no health insurance in Brazil, and I needed to get out of the decrepit state-run trauma unit into a private hospital. I ended up turning over my credit cards to my driver to manage the financial side of things until my husband arrived, and using Google Translate through voice command to communicate with my caregiver because I did not know the language.

One especially funny story that my husband and my representatives love to joke about is that once I was transferred to a private hospital, before my husband was due to arrive, I begged the nurses to please wash my hair and dry it. I didn't want my husband to see me with the mud, gravel, and blood in my hair from being thrown by the bus. I was more concerned about my physical appearance than anything else.

You Gain Acceptance

By sharing the lessons I'd learned and showing my vulnerability to my prospects and clients, I immediately put myself in a position of friend, opening up the platform for sharing freely and openly. As a business growth consultant, working with new and emerging entrepreneurs, I'm deeply involved in their businesses. As a result, my clients need to know that I'll hold their confidentiality close, and that they will not be condemned for something I may have not agreed with. By showing my vulnerability through my lessons learned, it makes it easier for them to take suggestions and advice to heart, knowing and believing that I am coming from a point of honesty and acceptance. I'm in this truly *with* them, and I want to see them succeed.

As entrepreneurs, it is imperative to understand the connection that must accompany the sales process. Whether dealing with new prospects or existing clients, you must remind yourself of *whom* is important in the process. It is *always* about the client, not you and your abilities. It is all about what you can do for them.

How can you help them solve their problems, given your experience and a value-based service or product offering?

GAINING STRENGTH THROUGH VULNER-ABILITY

Don't be afraid to make a fool of yourself — like the bit with my hair. Sometimes, it's the littlest things that demonstrate vulnerability more than anything. If they know that you can let loose with them, and really show who you are, they are going to be more drawn to you because of your credibility and openness.

Until recently, this would have been a difficult subject for me. Normally, one would consider strength and vulnerability as an oxymoron. However, what I've learned over the years — especially lately — is that showing vulnerability actually has strengthened my ability to connect with my clients on a much deeper level, and I close more deals because of it.

Vulnerability Removes Your Mask and Opens Your Eyes to Your True Self

Vulnerability is not easy. It is not something you can pretend to have. It requires self-assessment and introspection. I've tried the fake vulnerability act before, but learned that a prospect picks up on the lack of sincerity pretty quickly. It wasn't until my accident in Brazil that I truly understood where vulnerability comes from and how it could change my life and career immensely.

About four months after my accident, the blinders really came off, and I was forced to face my true self. I spoke earlier about the difficulty I previously had with vulnerability in the past, and the walls that I built to protect myself as I grew up. Those walls were actually my belief that I had only myself to count on to continue growing and moving forward in life.

The accident was just the beginning of dispelling those beliefs and forcing me to face the fact that I had to rely on others for help. Once the physical healing was well underway, and I was able to see the light at the end of the tunnel, I realized I was also suffering from the emotional effects of the accident, in the form of post-traumatic stress disorder (PTSD). I was going through a period of depression and put off getting out into the world again with my job. Understand: my job was in front of the public, speaking, selling, and networking. My sister, who was taking care of me when my husband was working during the day, told me that I needed to get counseling. She said she thought there were other issues going on that I did not even realize at the time.

I worked with a couple of psychiatrists — unsuccessfully. I finally met a consultant who specialized in PTSD and trauma. After a few weeks, it suddenly became clear why I was dragging my feet on getting back to my life. I was afraid of having to relive the accident every time someone asked me what had happened.

I don't remember the actual accident at all. The minute I saw the headlights of the bus and realized I could not move out of the way, I shut down. I don't remember anything from that moment until I was in the hospital, being wheeled into the trauma unit. The root cause of my PTSD was the fear that if someone asked me to tell what happened, I'd relive the accident, and the pain would resurface. I did not want to remember or feel that pain again. By blocking it, my mind was trying to protect me.

I needed to get over my PTSD in order to move forward. I needed to get out of my comfort zone, relive the accident, and talk about it. This realization opened my eyes and has become the topic of one of my keynote presentations.

After I returned home to the states, I found that somebody had videotaped the accident and posted it on YouTube, and my daughter had seen it. I refused to watch the video for fear of what I would see. As I continued working through my PTSD, it became clear that the only way I was going to break through the fear was to relive the accident.

You Gain Acceptance, Which Strengthens Your Resolve

Through understanding what was holding me back, I was able to uncover an even more important lesson: my fears were at the root of every one of my struggles not only in relation to my accident, but also throughout my life. Understanding this, and putting into practice an exercise of mindful examination to uncover the source of each of these challenges or doubts I face, I'm able to turn my negative thoughts around and gain strength by establishing a plan to overcome those fears.

As entrepreneurs—especially new and inexperienced ones—sales and finding customers are the primary underlying fears that you face. Lack of customers is also one of the main reasons businesses fail early on.

One key discriminant in successful entrepreneurial growth is that you can have the best product or service in the world, but without customers, there is no business. It's like being pregnant without a way to deliver. When a business depends on customers to grow, it stands to reason that the fear of selling can cripple a company. By facing the fear and examining where this fear is coming from, you can turn that fear around to your advantage. By being vulnerable, and showing a genuine connection, the positive energy that you put out to the universe comes back many times more. Customers pick up on it, and are attracted to what you, as an entrepreneur, are offering.

An example of how acceptance of your vulnerability can lead to strength is that I'm currently involved in a long-term project based around medical tourism. I've been invited to participate as part of the development team focusing on the marketing and branding side of medical tourism. Although I understand the medical tourism side of the business, I know just enough to be dangerous. Naturally, the fears I face are my lack of thorough understanding and experience within the industry. I have to remind myself that there's a reason I was asked to participate as part of this early-stage development team. Adding to my apprehension is that, as part of this team, I'm dealing with very high-level individuals with much more experience than I have.

But is that stopping me?

Absolutely not. Knowing the origin of my anxiety and fears, I actively gain the understanding and knowledge needed to move forward with this project.

You're Able to Offer More of Yourself to Others

As a new entrepreneur, you tend to wear many hats. Another reason that many new businesses fail early on is burnout. Through accepting and understanding that you can't do it all, and by reaching out and surrounding yourself with the experts and knowledgeable resources needed to succeed, you truly can move forward. Along with efficient delegation of responsibilities in a growing business comes the understanding of the need for work-life balance. It's so easy to get so wrapped up in your new business that you forget about everything else. Being a good entrepreneur of a growing company involves more than skill. It requires a healthy emotional and physical balance, as well. If there is not a healthy balance, burnout can creep in and rob your passion and drive to operate the business.

When I began my second business, which ultimately failed, I realized too late that I had gotten into it for all the wrong reasons. It was a ceramic business that manufactured lamps for the hospitality industry. I always loved ceramics; I had enjoyed dabbling in ceramics all my life. I thought that operating a business around something I loved was the best of both worlds.

I purchased the business from a friend who was suffering from cancer, believing that I was relieving her from a burden while she was struggling with this debilitating illness. I quickly realized that I had bitten off more than I could chew. Not only did I not have the business acumen needed to run a business, I didn't know anything about manufacturing, either. I got into this business for the wrong reasons and did not have the skill level to make it a success.

Shortly after I bought the business, I was spending countless hours at the shop, struggling to fill orders while learning all I needed to learn about the business. I realized I hated working with ceramics. My long hours working within a dusty, hot, and dirty environment eventually had a terrible effect on my health and my mental clarity. One day, while working in the glazing area, the belt for the compressor for the glazing gun began to slip because of all the dust. Stupidly, I tried to start the belt with my hand, and the belt ultimately pulled my hand through, catching my finger and amputating the top part of my right ring finger.

I know you're probably thinking: *What a really stupid thing to do.*

You would be absolutely right, but I was tired, burned out, and frustrated. If I hadn't been, I probably would have been able to reason with myself and made a better choice. The doctors were able to save about 70 percent of my finger through extensive surgery and hyperbolic treatment to get the blood flowing again, but because the business depended on me—and I was out of work for weeks recuperating—we ended up closing the doors, and I have not worked in ceramics again since then.

As an entrepreneur, there is only so much that you can do and only so much of you to go around. You need to recognize your limitations, hire others to assist, or strategically partner with others to strengthen your value.

Understand that vulnerability is not a weakness. Vulnerability is a strength. It not only strengthens your relationships personally, but also in your business. With your family, children, friends, and colleagues, let them see that you're a real person. You don't have to be an expert at everything.

I tried to be a supermom and live up to that ideal for so long. It doesn't work. No one is a supermom. No one is perfect.

LEAVING A LEGACY

When we talk about leaving a legacy, that's what work-life balance is all about. This is leaving a legacy. As human beings, it's in your DNA to want to make a difference in the world before you leave it, whether it is for your children or grandchildren, or even something bigger that impacts many more people. Your legacy is a direct reflection of your ultimate dreams, as entrepreneurs and as human beings. Your legacy represents the ultimate in vulnerability; it demonstrates your true desires. Without a legacy, your purpose for living and engaging in day-to-day life becomes obsolete and meaningless.

Family

As a mother of two grown adults and a grandmother of three, naturally I want to leave a legacy with them of being a strong, formidable, loving wife, mother, and grandmother. Furthermore, I would love to leave this world having known I made an impact on their lives; that I have made their lives easier, either financially or otherwise. More than anything, I want to leave them with the skills and tools that I have learned over a lifetime that they can use and grow with, so that they can make informed, strategic decisions that will impact their futures and enable them to leave their own legacy later on.

A Message

Your legacy may apply to your personal life or your business life. As far as I'm concerned, the message I want to build and leave as I move forward is that every one of us has the ability and passion within us to take control of our own lives, whether it's as entrepreneurs or staying in the corporate environment as employees. The way that you do that is by facing your fears and drawing strength from them, and getting to the root of what's causing them and turning them around. However, the dream is only part of the message. The rest involves imparting the skills, tools, and knowledge entrepreneurs need to succeed in their endeavors.

A Platform to Build On

The lessons you've learned along the way ultimately become the platform for building a legacy. When you think about it, your lessons make up the legacy you leave behind. In your personal life, they can be the stories you bring into the family — the folklore — that causes them to think and remember what family is. On the business side, the term *legacy* takes on a whole other meaning. For me, the legacy that I want to leave with my company is the impact that I hope to make on the number of failed businesses each year in the United States. Although it's a huge dream, with the right help and systematic planning, I believe that my efforts and dreams could spread throughout the nation, as a large team of people who share my dream are born out of this effort and live to carry on this message and dream.

A platform to build on is a living environment. It continues to grow. It continues to feed generation after generation. If you are the one to start that legacy, you want to make sure you put into place the structure that's needed to make that happen.

Call to Action!

If you are thinking of starting a side business or *side-hustle* as it is known today, you might want to watch our webinar *"Are You A HOBO"* (*Hobby Owner or Business Owner*) for some tips on how to grow your side-hustle into something more substantial. Go to www.marketatomy.com/bktools for details.

CHAPTER THREE

The Fears That Hold Us Back

THE ROOT OF ALL YOUR OBSTACLES ARE YOUR FEARS

Awareness is key to understanding. As an entrepreneur, you jump into business with both feet. You immerse yourself completely toward a common goal, which is to succeed and make money. You initially put blinders on to the downside of entrepreneurship until it hits you square in the face. Then all of a sudden, your passion takes a direct hit, and you begin to question your reasons for going into business in the first place.

Entrepreneurship is not all a bed of roses, or even the answer to your lifelong dream, or the path to gaining control over your financial future. There will be obstacles that will challenge your resolve, make you question your dreams and capabilities, and second-guess your actions. Understanding this going in is half the battle to overcoming these obstacles.

The other half is knowing:

1. Where are these obstacles coming from?
2. How can you break through them?

Getting to the Root of Your Fears

We're all born into this world without any notion of fear. We trust implicitly and don't question the world around us. In general, life ushers in your fear. Before you know it, you end up harboring a boatload of self-doubt, anxiety, and insecurities that hold you back from being the best person you can be.

As an adult, you tend to either ignore your fears or don't realize they're even there, lying dormant in your unconscious mind, until one day —*bam!*—something, like being hit by a bus, triggers the fear and brings it front and center. Without even realizing it, you develop a strong shell around yourself to protect you from having to face your fears, just so you can move through life behind a mask of strength, confidence, and false security. But when things get challenging, as they do when starting a business, you tend to hold yourself back for fear of failure and making a fool of yourself.

I have reinvented myself so many times after each epic failure or setback in my forty-plus year career that when I started my own business in 2009, the image I chose to represent my company was a phoenix. I could relate personally to the concept of starting anew; a new life, stronger, more secure, moving forward. Out of the ashes of my most recent tragedy rose a new me, ready to take on the world and prove to everyone around me I was okay. Deep down, however, I had serious doubts about my life's purpose.

Throughout my adult working life, I felt that by demonstrating my capabilities and my abilities to my employers, they in turn would see the value I brought to their business, and would reward me in kind. That wasn't the case.

I was just a means to an end, a cog in a wheel. As I stated earlier, I have two failed businesses behind me. Each time I felt underappreciated and frustrated with my current career path, I would jump on the entrepreneurship bandwagon, only to go down in flames because I really was not prepared to go out on my own. The dreams of taking control of my career and life were not good reasons to leap into entrepreneurship.

In 2009, when I was first laid off from my position with a major construction management firm, my fears of incompetence threatened to derail me. Fortunately, I have a very compassionate husband who has an innate knack for quickly putting things in perspective. He took me away for the weekend, stating that nothing was going to change before we returned the following

Monday. I could tackle my next challenge then. What happened when we did return was the catalyst to set me on the path to where I am today.

Understanding Fear

When faced with challenges in life, sometimes all we want to do is shut ourselves off. After my layoff, I was angry and ashamed. I had spent the last two and a half years married to my work for an organization, only to have them throw me out like an old shoe.

Let me explain something: the reason cited for my layoff was not economic reasons, but rather because of an error I had made in my last proposal response. Now for the backstory: at the time I was hired with the same firm, I had been working in the industry for almost twenty-eight years in marketing, sales, and strategic planning. It was the architectural, engineering, and construction industry, but we'll call it the AEC industry. I had managed to work within, and learn, every logistical stage within the AEC industry. My value that I brought to this firm was the understanding of all the stages in the process, and how to market to and within the various stages.

As I stated earlier, when I started my new job, I was immediately faced with unexpected challenges in the form of nonexistent systems that would make my job impossible to manage in a timely and efficient manner. I had to hit the ground running without the resources needed to rise to the occasion.

So what did I do?

Instead of backing down, I spent the next six months developing an organizing system that would allow me to streamline my department and manage the various tasks and responsibilities I needed to get done. At the time of my hiring, I had an assistant working with me, which allowed me to delegate and move through this process. That was, until she was let go, due reportedly to budget cutbacks. The timing coincided with the peak of the most recent recession. At the same time, we were processing an average of approximately sixty to sixty-five proposal responses each year, along with the other responsibilities, which was a level we could handle as long as I had an assistant to help me.

My anxiety level the week before I was let go was through the roof. I was working an average of seventy to eighty hours a week, turning out one and a half proposals *by myself* each week. The average time it took me to respond was approximately twenty-four to thirty hours per response. This didn't even include my other marketing responsibilities. I had warned my boss that unless they got me help, mistakes were going to happen. This was a fear I had. It so happened that on the fateful day of my termination, one of the responses submitted on a major project was missing a key piece of information.

Because of my fears that something would go wrong, we had implemented checks and balances to double-check my work. Unfortunately, two other reviewers of the final submission missed the same thing I did. It wasn't as though the item was left out or ignored. It was sitting on the counter, signed and ready to go; it just didn't make it into the final, completed document. Needless to say, I was called on the carpet for my oversight, and at that point, I was exhausted. I had had enough, and we worked out an agreement in which I was able to leave and collect unemployment.

Accepting That Fears Are Legitimate

First, it's important to understand that often fears are rooted in something deeper. Often, the source of fear is centered on a lack of understanding. As an entrepreneur, the obstacles you encounter are primarily based on your fears that you don't know what you're doing and that you'll screw up.

When I first started that job and realized that things were not as they had been presented, I spoke up. I panicked. I felt that I was being set up for failure from the very beginning — failure being one of my biggest fears. But that didn't stop me from turning things around and making the best of a rotten situation.

I had the basic knowledge of what needed to be done, but lacked the understanding of where to begin to seek the resources needed to move forward. As I've said, knowledge is power. Through better understanding, you can accept and challenge your fears and break through them.

After being laid off and spending a wonderful weekend away with my husband, I returned to an onslaught of well-meaning voicemail messages from friends and family reaching out to me. Some colleagues were going through similar situations. Some of my colleagues, with whom I'd been working closely for the previous two and a half years, were just as blindsided by my exit as I was.

At the same time, we were at the peak of one of the largest recessions to hit the United States, or the world for that matter. I had seen the writing on the wall. I knew that eventually I would be laid off. It had just come sooner than I had planned. But because of this foresight, my husband and I had already started the process of venturing out with our own business prior to my layoff; it boiled down to a matter of identifying what the business was going to be. I did not want to return to the corporate environment again, primarily because I was tired of having to bust my butt for an organization that had no appreciation of the value I brought to the company.

By this time, I had received my business marketing degree and had a better understanding of what to expect and prepare for this time around as an entrepreneur. This is where the next stage of my career took hold. Knowing the dire situation within the country and the world, I decided that I needed to create my own job. I needed to figure out where I fit, based on my talents and abilities.

How could I make a difference in my life and impact those I encountered along the way?

My research at the time revealed that Brazil was the only country gaining strength in the downed global economy. This was primarily because it was a cash country, and it had recently been awarded the 2014 *Fédération Internationale de Football Association* (FIFA) games and the 2016 Summer Olympic games. I considered what this meant for a struggling AEC industry, and how I could contribute to opening up the Brazilian market.

I developed a business model that would allow me to travel to Brazil and create inroads for U.S. companies seeking to break into the Brazilian market. Now, although I understood the logistical lifecycle of the

AEC industry and knew the timeline that was getting ready to break loose in Brazil because of the upcoming international events, I had never worked on that scale and did not know what to expect crossing borders into Brazil. So my apprehension and fear level was through the roof at that point.

But I knew that I needed to identify the source of my fear. I needed to explore my apprehension with moving forward.

CONFRONT YOUR FEARS TO GET PAST THEM

Burying your fears will only allow them to grow stronger. By confronting your fears, you become stronger as an individual, ushering in the ability to move forward. As entrepreneurs, it is important to understand that in order to grow, you have to be able to first identify the obstacles in the way. This is why the first challenge with any entrepreneurship involves understanding where the fears lie—the weaknesses—and where your strengths are to overcome them.

In the business world, this has long been known as a SWOT analysis:

- Strengths
- Weaknesses
- Opportunities
- Threats

A SWOT analysis examines the business strengths and weaknesses internally, as well as the opportunities and threats externally that could hurt or help your chances for success.

The SWOT premise can apply to your personal life as well. By examining where your strengths lie currently, and what fears you harbor that could circumvent your efforts from moving forward in life, you can effectively develop a strategy for breaking through any barriers that could hold you back. The same goes for any opportunities or threats that could have a direct impact on your life.

There are opportunities that could drastically change the trajectory of your life for the positive, but because of your fears, you may not see these opportunities for what they are.

Examples of some of these changes include:

- Weddings
- Births
- Career changes

As far as threats, there are certain life challenges that you have absolutely no control over:

- Death
- Illness
- Loss of a job

Understanding that *life happens* is only part of the equation. Having a process to work through these events is the other part.

Face Them Where They Are

As I said before, knowledge is key to overcoming the obstacles in life and in business. This is the primary reason I developed the MarketAtomy concept for entrepreneurs. Here are the sobering statistics that I repeat several times throughout this book, because I really want you to understand them. According to the U.S. Small Business Association, more than five hundred thousand new businesses start each year within the United States; 85 percent of these businesses fail within the first two years.

After my efforts in Brazil started to slow down because of their own economic recession and political issues in 2013, I realized that, once again, I had to reevaluate where I was going with my company. At the same time, friends and colleagues were starting to come to me. They had started their own businesses during the previous recession in the United States because they couldn't find jobs. They were concerned because they couldn't seem to break through the invisible revenue ceiling or had trouble attracting and retaining customers.

When asked what strategies and procedures they had in place for their companies, more often than not, there weren't any. They had no business plans, no marketing strategies, and no sales plans. They were merely providing a service or product without a road map or a goal in mind. They had a good product or service, but lacked basic business knowledge and the knowhow of how to attract and engage customers. I liken it to being pregnant without a way to deliver.

I saw them mortgaging their homes and depleting their retirement accounts to keep a business funded that they really had no business having started in the first place. It broke my heart to see them losing their shirts, merely because they lacked the knowledge to understand what was needed to succeed. I quickly realized that I needed to concentrate my efforts stateside, to develop a program that would help them and other new entrepreneurs in the same situation.

Develop a Strategy

Birthing a business is a laborious and scary undertaking. Not only do you fight the external influences that could make or break the new business, you also fight the internal battles that bring out every fear that has been deeply ingrained in your psyche. There is a process in building a business, just like there is a process in life. It begins with a dream, and it's in the dream stage that a seed is waiting to be nurtured. The nurturing comes with research and knowledge. Just like birthing a baby, you have the gestational period that involves the dream and development of the conceptualization. Then you move into the delivery, or the birth of the business. Finally, you have to raise that business from infancy to maturity. None of this happens without knowledge.

Just like in life, there are a lot of different viewpoints on what to expect when expecting a child. There are also a lot of different opinions on what to expect when expecting and growing a business. The MarketAtomy concept is visually built around the human body to illustrate the infrastructure that needs to be in place to build and grow a healthy business. Hence the name, marketing plus anatomy: MarketAtomy.

MarketAtomy is designed to alleviate the unknown and to prepare new entrepreneurs for what to expect through the various stages of growing a business. It demonstrates that marketing and branding are the heart of every business. This is the WHY you are in business.

Why holds the answers to:

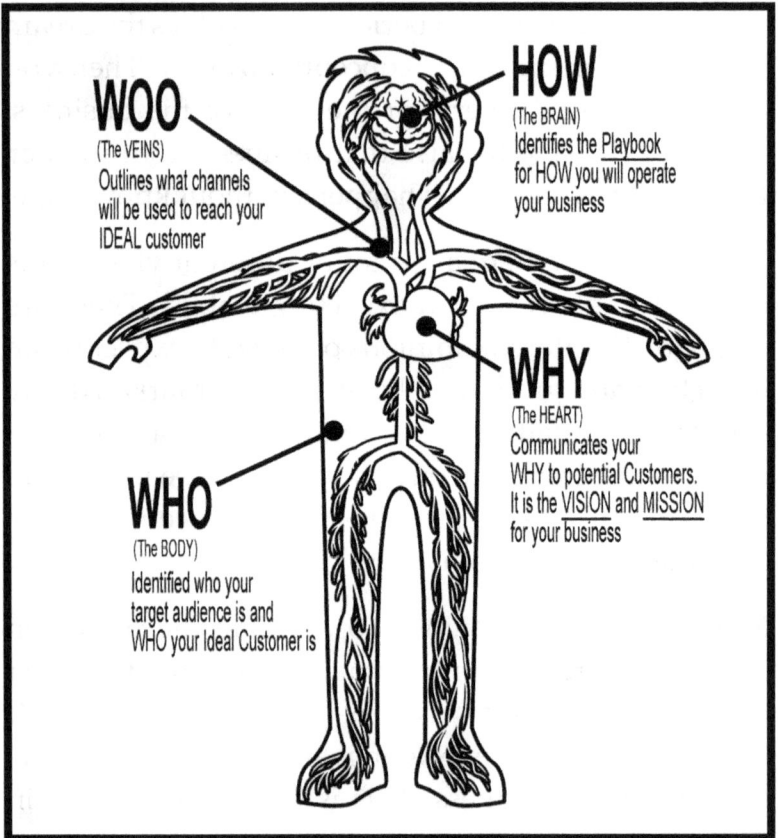

WOO
(The VEINS)
Outlines what channels will be used to reach your IDEAL customer

HOW
(The BRAIN)
Identifies the Playbook for HOW you will operate your business

WHY
(The HEART)
Communicates your WHY to potential Customers. It is the VISION and MISSION for your business

WHO
(The BODY)
Identified who your target audience is and WHO your Ideal Customer is

- Your motivation
- Vision
- The mission behind starting the business in the first place

All the strategic plans are located in what we can think of as the brain of your business venture, such as:

- Business plan
- Pricing strategy
- Marketing strategy
- Your product or service

They answer the question of HOW you are going to run your business.

Just like in the human body, the heart and brain must work in tandem to communicate to the body to move, eat, or love.

In the MarketAtomy concept, the heart and brain work together to send out the marketing message through the veins, or the tools used to WOO your ideal customer, or your WHO. These are your potential customers. This seems like a very simple concept, but when seen in its entirety, one quickly realizes that the product or service you went into business with in the first place is just one small component located within the brain. Without all of these other working elements, the message is not communicated to the market, resulting in lack of awareness and no customers. Without customers, there is no business.

Just Go for It

Fear of failure is one of the biggest challenges to stepping out and grabbing the brass ring of entrepreneurship, as I've stated before. Understanding the root of that fear of failure is key to moving forward. Sometimes it takes a leap of faith and trust that the process will be discovered on the way down.

When the decision was made to explore breaking into the Brazilian market, there was definite apprehension on my part. First, I had never done business internationally before in my life. Second, I had never traveled internationally without my husband. I was fighting a fear of exploring the unknown and my fear of leaving behind my safety net. However, I trusted enough in my knowledge of the AEC environment, the processes involved, and the timeline that was before me. I took that leap of faith, decided to pull up my big-girl panties, and just did it.

If I didn't, I would have always wondered: *What if?*

That is one of the worst regrets to ever have in the long term. I decided that even if nothing came of this endeavor, the experience alone was worth the investment.

I spent the first year just learning what Brazil needed to prepare for the upcoming games. What I found out was much more than I had expected. Once I had determined what was needed, and began creating the inroads, I traveled back three more times that year merely to research where I would fit into what was currently happening within Brazil.

Once I had a solid plan I came back to the United States and proceeded to find the solutions to meet their needs. My business model allowed me to get these clients to the decision makers in Brazil without them having to spend a whole bunch of money on international expansion. Also as an added benefit, I was introduced firsthand to some of the newest technological advances, products, systems, and processes within the AEC environment worldwide.

Hesitation is another of the biggest roadblocks to entrepreneurship. The root of hesitation is buried in fear: the fear of failure. The "what if?" syndrome can haunt you for the rest of your life. Imagine what feelings would crop up a few months or years down the road, when your idea suddenly emerges under someone else's name. Risk is part of the process of entrepreneurship. Mitigating that risk is also part of the process.

Mitigation stems from:

- Knowledge
- Acceptance of what your limits are
- Reaching out to others when needed

Earlier, I mentioned that I believe there's an entrepreneur in every one of us. You need to identify what it is that you're passionate about, and not allow your fears to hold you back.

ENLIGHTENMENT

This is one of my favorite subjects, because this is what comes out of the entrepreneurial process. As I've reiterated many times, knowledge paves the way for enlightenment. You cannot have your eyes opened unless you understand what you are seeking. Acceptance of your limitations is the first key to understanding. None of us is expected to have all the answers. I don't care how talented, educated, or aware you are; you never stop learning.

The best lessons are lessons learned by others.

Those of us who have failed and continue to try are full of lessons learned that others can benefit from and capitalize on. As entrepreneurs it is critical that we spread our knowledge and expertise to help others avoid the same mistakes we have already made.

MarketAtomy was birthed out of lessons not only in building and growing a business, but also in self-awareness and physical healing. Entrepreneurship involves more than skill. Understanding the emotional ties, both personally and professionally, are extremely important in uncovering the fears or obstacles holding you back.

Additionally, entrepreneurship can take a very big toll on your health if you are not careful. It is important to remain physically fit in order to manage the day-to-day stress involved in owning your own business. It's a holistic approach that involves the mind, body, and soul. Your passion is what drives the dream. *You* are the one behind the wheel. Y*our soul* is ingrained into every aspect of your business. Keeping it healthy is your number-one goal.

Breaking Through Is a Process

None of this happens overnight. Understanding the process and managing the layers can be daunting. However, think back to when you attended college, or even high school for that matter. One of the first things you had to do was determine what career path you wanted. This represents the goal, or the endgame. Then you had to determine a pathway to achieving that goal or entering that career. This involved laying out your course schedule for the next three to four years and ensuring that all prerequisites were met before you could move onto the next step. This is what it takes to build a business.

Building a business is not a linear approach; it is all over the place, and flexibility is key. This understanding is also what it takes to break through the fears and obstacles that hold you back. You have to first understand where you want to get to, then figure out what is holding you back and what is triggering the fear. Once you have determined where that root lies, you can develop a strategy to break through or bypass it to get to the other side.

When I was fighting back after my accident in Brazil, my pride stood in the way of my progress. I felt I was fine before the accident, so I thought the reason I couldn't move forward had to be something that involved the accident, not something from earlier in my life that I had been holding onto. I fought the process, until one day I was forced to face my fear.

The ultimate fear that stood in my way was loss of control. I felt that my entire early life had been controlled by someone or something else. As a result, I found myself constantly fighting against this control. I would do or say stupid things to demonstrate that I had control.

It wasn't until I could accept that I can't control everything that my business and personal relationships turned around. These control issues extended as far back as I could remember. To this day, I can't tell you when the fear of not being in control of my life began, but I know that it has governed every major decision I have ever made. It wasn't until this accident, when I was forced to hand over control to my representatives, the doctors and nurses, my caregivers, and everyone else for almost six months of my life that I realized life went on even when I wasn't controlling everything.

The Other Side Holds the Dream

It all boils down to one thing: the dream is what keeps you motivated and moving ahead. As long as you hold onto the dream, the world doesn't appear as daunting.

It might seem as though you are always looking through rose-colored classes, but hey, you need a little color in your life, right?

The key to holding onto a dream is to share it with those around you. As you engage them in your dreams, you're never alone.

American poet Langston Hughes wrote a poem called "Hold Fast to Dreams." In this poem, Hughes writes, "Life is a broken-winged bird/That cannot fly." This is a poem that resonates with me and reminds me that even though one of my biggest fears is of losing control, I always retain control of my dreams. No one can take those away from me.

Those Particular Fears Disappear

One of the things I've become aware of through all my journeys, especially those of late, is that once confronted, accepted, and overcome, those fears never crop up again. There are healthy fears and unhealthy fears. You want to hold onto the healthy fears, naturally, but the unhealthy fears are what I'm talking about here.

When confronted with the unexpected, the natural instinct is to back away from the fear; that's called *avoidance*. You know the drill. Some part of you wants to curl up into a fetal position and rely on hope that something will turn out for the better. I can tell you that I would shut down. I'd curl up in bed and tell myself that tomorrow was another day; I could start fresh then. That was avoidance, because I wasn't overcoming the fear. I was just tucking it back away. How you respond to challenges is how you respond in life, love, and work. If you teach yourself to shut down, so will it be in other areas of your life.

Enlightenment, like I said, is one of my favorite topics. When consulting with my clients, I've frequently seen that when they sit down and do their business modeling and financial modeling sessions, all of the sudden their eyes light up.

Clients realize, "Oh, gosh, this is a real business! It was always in my head, but all of the sudden, it seems real!"

They're seeing numbers. They're seeing the actual makeup of their business. Unless you can sit down and put your fears in front of you, just like getting your business out of your head and down on paper in front of you, you're going to continue to be held back. Like you, the minute these clients see their businesses in front of them in black and white, they see their pathway to success.

Call to Action!

An effective way of reducing your fears is knowledge. Typically you fear what you don't feel you are knowledgeable about. We have an assessment that tests your entrepreneurial skills and even offers insight as to what you might need to work on to grow into the entrepreneur you wish to be. Additionally, we will be launching the MarketAtomy eLearning platform in 2017 to help you gaining the knowledge you need. For more info, go to www.marketatomy.com/bktools.

CHAPTER FOUR

The MarketAtomy
Concept Expanded

MARKETING AND BRANDING ARE THE HEART OF ANY BUSINESS

Birthing a business involves more than just a good product or service. You can have the best product or service in the world, but without customers, there is no business. There are many components that make up a successful business, all of which interact to provide a solid infrastructure for attracting, selling, and servicing the customer. But at the heart of every activity — every message — is marketing and branding. It's the DNA of your business.

Just like a baby carries the DNA of each its parents, your business carries the DNA of your thoughts, your passions, and your *why*. Just like a baby enters the world with its own distinct set of physical and emotional characteristics, your business is presented to the marketplace with its own unique selling proposition (USP). That's what makes your company different, and this is what your marketing and branding communicates to the market.

Branding Brings Awareness

Think about it:

Who are you?

What makes you an individual?

Think back to when you were in elementary school, and imagine yourself out on the playground, all by yourself, and another kid comes up and asks you to play.

What was it in you that drew that kid to you?

First impressions are critical in the branding process. How you back up that first impression is what keeps that kid coming back to become a lifelong friend. Your brand is what makes you instantly recognizable. It's the thing that represents who, what, and why you are who you are. It's more important than your personality or your physical characteristics. It's your morality. It's the compassion and the behavioral traits that make you *you*.

The same can be said for your business. Your brand in business is more than your logo or slogan. It's how you identify with your customers, even to the point of how they feel doing business with you. Your brand is the reputation you have in the market, and the culture you build within your company from the experiences both internally and externally.

Walt Disney was all about branding; not only from the iconic Mickey Mouse image, but also in the way he treated his employees, and the lasting experiences he left in the minds of his customers. A brand can supersede the present. Just like stories and images passed down through generations of family members leaving a legacy, a brand can dictate and drive customers' experiences long before they actually come in contact with the brand and remain long after.

"It's a Small World After All" is a brand.

"When You Wish Upon a Star" is a brand.

How many can say that they don't know the rest of the words to the song?

Makes no difference who you are.

Anything your heart desires will come to you.

Walt Disney wanted to create a place where people young and old could come and enjoy themselves, just for a little while, leaving the rest of the world outside. I worked for Disney during my young teen years. It's difficult to work in an environment like Disney World and not have it rub off on you to some degree. Even now, decades later, I look back at my experience as an employee with awe at the level of imagination this man brought to the world. It's important to remember that your brand is *you*, as its designer, its cheerleader, and its parent.

Marketing Speaks

Marketing is the voice behind your brand. It is how you communicate to the world the message that you want customers to hear. It's difficult for new entrepreneurs to grasp the concept of marketing and creating awareness. Awareness is what attracts prospects, who ultimately turn into customers. The primary purpose of marketing is to communicate your brand message to the market and potential customers.

In preparation of my travels to Brazil to explore opportunities for the U.S. AEC industry, I had to strategically develop my plan for creating awareness and interest in the products and services my clients had to offer. My brand message was to position myself as a bridge between U.S. and Brazilian AEC firms to introduce new and efficient systems, processes, and products that would streamline the development process in preparation for the upcoming FIFA and Olympic games.

Before I did that, however, I had to understand the Brazilian market; for instance, what areas they needed help with and what it would take to penetrate the market. All of these activities were part of the marketing process, in the form of market research. This is what I did the first twelve months in Brazil. It's all about knowing whom you're marketing to, and uncovering the best way reach them so that they can connect with you and your services.

In its infancy, my relationship with Brazil was daunting. During the first year of discovery, I was able to uncover their biggest *pain points*, as they related to the design-and-build side of the industry, in preparation for the upcoming games. I was then able to return to the United States and find a solution for their needs. Although I was representing several U.S. firms within the Brazilian market, the brand I was continuously portraying was one of an expert in providing new and improved AEC solutions.

Eventually, my brand took on a life of its own as we grew within the Brazilian market. Ultimately, my brand became recognized as one of the new technology solution providers among the industry in Brazil. None of this could have happened if my marketing message had not been established early on, and my efforts had not been focused on one outcome: attracting customers, albeit for my clients, but ultimately for my company as well. My reputation was on the line with my brand.

Communicate the Message

First of all, effectively communicating the marketing message is critical to engaging the end user, or your prospect, and if all goes well, ultimately your customer. There are so many channels you can use to communicate your marketing message. There are both inbound and outbound marketing tools that deliver your message out to your ideal customer. I like to call them your WOO. This is how you reach and attract potential customers, how you WOO them. The message, however, should be impactful, clear, and concise. It should come from the heart, your brand, and speak directly to your customer.

I had to demonstrate consistency to the people in Brazil by returning until they felt comfortable that I would deliver. I had to continuously demonstrate the level of technology and systems that I could provide along with solutions to make the process smooth and transparent. I also needed to establish a moral and ethical backbone that stood strong in the face of corruption.

Consider the pharmaceutical industry. You've seen the television ads promoting various pharmaceutical products, and the benefits associated with those products. Then, immediately, they're followed up with the potential side effects.

By the time the commercial has ended, I'm thinking: *My reason for trying this new product would have to be pretty dire for me to subject myself to the potential side effects that come with it. For that matter, do we know what the product being advertised was for?*

So many of these pharmaceutical advertisements are vague about the symptoms and diseases that they treat. I understand that there are methods to their madness, but being on the receiving end of these messages is not only confusing, but depressing as well.

The purpose of your message is to communicate your passion, and the benefits of your product or service in a clear, concise manner that speaks directly to your target audience.

The message should speak directly to your audience and their pain point. How can you relieve their pain?

Although I could not relate to the various pharmaceutical advertisements, I am sure there are those who could. These are the customers they're targeting, the ones who can feel an attachment to the products being advertised.

THE BRAIN HOLDS THE PLAYBOOK FOR YOUR BUSINESS

Everything that you know, everything that you think, comes from your brain. You need a brain to stay alive; without it, you'd be dead, which is why *brain dead* is the legal definition of death. Scientifically, someone is brain dead when there is a lack of reflexive responsive control by the brain stem, which is at the core of the brain, controlling the vital functions of the body. However, the brain is not exclusive in its ability to maintain life. It is merely the mechanism for communicating to the other vital organs what needs to be done.

In business, the brain holds the playbook of instructions needed to run your business.

These instructions include several elements:

- A business plan
- A marketing strategy
- A pricing strategy for your products and service
- The makeup of your product and service offerings

The brain of your business is the Holy Grail. Without it, it's like trying to operate a car without understanding the process of inserting the key into the ignition. You have to start the car, put it in gear to make the vehicle move, and know how and when to stop before you hit something.

The Details Are the Plan

Imagine you're playing baseball with one of your favorite teams. However, none of the team positions are identified; it's just a free-for-all. Anybody can play any position they desire, whether they are good or not. There would be total chaos. There would be positions that were unfilled, positions that were filled to overcapacity, or maybe filled by someone who was not a good fit for that position.

The strategic plans that you put in place for your business are the organizational activities — the details and priorities — that you have determined are at the core of your brand. They outline the details on how customers are treated, what you charge for your products or services, and who is responsible for certain tasks or areas. Your strategic plans ensure that your business can operate as a unified entity, as opposed to chaos.

While growing up, we have certain rules enforced upon us as children that we are expected to follow. Some of these rules are to protect us, like not crossing the street before looking both ways, or not touching a hot burner on the stove. Some of the rules are meant to guide us, like treating others as we would like to be treated, or accepting responsibility for something that we did that hurt someone else.

Then there are those steadfast rules, governed by forces out of the immediate family environment, such as, "Thou shalt not kill" or "Thou shalt not commit adultery."

Some of these may be enforced by law; others by beliefs and morality.

The rules for business follow the same guidelines.

There are those that are controlled within the business environment, such as:

- The product or service makeup
- The price point for the product or service
- The experience you want your customer to receive whenever they make a purchase from you

There are also rules that are designed to guide you, but over which you have no control, such as:

- Amount and due date for taxes
- Rules regarding comingling your business and personal finances

The point is that in business, the guiding rules and regulations should be identified up front and governed accordingly. This is all controlled in the brain function of the business.

The Plan Is the Road Map

Some of the strategic plan functions identified in the brain involve a process for accomplishing the task identified in the rules. My efforts in Brazil involved a series of processes. For example, since I had never traveled to Brazil before, I had to make sure I had the documentation in place to be able to travel there for business. I had to make sure that I had my accommodations and other necessary details identified and taken care of before I even booked my airline ticket. These were all processes that led me down a path to the point where I made my first trip into Brazil, knowing that I had a fairly good idea of what was expected of me, and what I could expect of my environment.

In business, the first part of the growth process for success involves understanding where you're going. Otherwise, you won't know when you arrive. Once you have the beginning and end points, filling in the road map becomes clearer. By breaking down the pathway into smaller components, you're able to identify measurable milestones that confirm the forward momentum you have set in place for your business, which allows you the opportunity to celebrate your successes along the way.

The Guidebook for Doing

Developing the strategic plan and road map is one part, but they're useless if the systems are not implemented. Taking action is key. As a consultant, one of the things I hear more often than anything else is that the plan has already been developed, but it's either been sitting on a shelf for the past five years, or it's been sitting in the owner's brain and hasn't been put on paper.

What good does the plan do for your business if it's sitting on a shelf?

Your business is stagnant. You're not moving forward. If you're not taking action, you're not growing your business.

When my kids were little, they would do their homework but often leave it sitting on the table when they left for school.

Why do all the hard work, only to throw it away?

They did the work, but still earned an incomplete because they didn't take the last step, which was to hand it in. It's important that the action be behind the plan. If you can't keep that momentum moving forward, you're going to stagnate and the business will die.

THE HEART AND THE BRAIN WORK IN TANDEM

The MarketAtomy concept came to me a couple of years ago, when I was working with small and emerging companies. As stated earlier, the reason I came up with the concept was because I found that these entrepreneurs were investing a lot of money into failed businesses, and the businesses were failing because they didn't have the knowledge needed to operate them. I decided to develop something that was visually graphic to show them how to set up and run these businesses, and what needed to be in place in order for them to grow and succeed. I built it around the human body, because that always has been relevant to me in understanding the concept.

The MarketAtomy concept is related to the human body, primarily the heart and brain, and how they must work in tandem to maintain the body's vital functions. Branding and marketing must work in tandem with the strategic plans established for your business to keep the business growing and functioning.

Neither One of Them Can Survive on Their Own

As in the human body, the brain cannot survive without the heart feeding it the blood and oxygen needed to keep it functioning. At the same time, the strategic processes identified within the brain of the organization cannot function without the message and brand fed to it through the heart of the business. In order to carry out the strategy of attracting customers, you need the brand and marketing message to convey the benefits the customer would receive, as well as to determine the marketing channels to be utilized in the outreach process. To ensure that customer experience expectations are met, employees and service personnel also need to understand what the brand message is, and how it relates to them and their jobs.

The two functions work in tandem. If the strategies are not in place, the message cannot be communicated and delivered. If marketing and branding efforts are eliminated, prospects can't know or understand the benefits or values that your firm offers, and how you can help them solve their problem.

One Provides Passion; the Other Provides Information

Passion is one of the most effective motivators when it comes to launching a business, and often one of the strongest predictors of whether an idea will lead to success, according to billionaire Richard Branson, founder of the Virgin Group. Business is driven by passion. That passion is what is communicated through the marketing and branding message. The passion is fed into the strategic plan in the brain, so that the strategic plan can be carried out through the organization and the market. Launching a business simply to make money is a guaranteed disaster. It lacks the relationships and passion needed to grow. Rather than a positive brand message that draws customers in, you end up with a brand that pushes them away. Without customers, there's really no business. When you compare a business to the human body, all of the knowledge is up in the brain. The heart is what holds the passion, love, and compassion for others.

It's the Fuel That Drives the Business

First of all, a right-thinking and creative frame of mind is all it takes to achieve anything you desire. Being persistent in business will only make it easier to achieve your goals. That forward momentum is what you need to keep moving toward your goals. Business is a domain that is unpredictable, and so is life. You don't know the end result, but if you have a clear vision of the journey and what it is that you want to get out of your business, then you're pointed in the right direction to achieve success.

It's important that you find ways to keep the passion alive. The marketing and branding message need to be focused, and they need to be driven out into the market. That is what creates the momentum. There are also other ways that you need to continue to create that momentum; not only the marketing and branding activities, but you need to keep your mind and your emotions involved as well, through coaching and mentoring. Some of the world's leading sports figures and CEOs engage their own professional coaches to keep them on track and on target.

Through the MarketAtomy concept, it's important for new entrepreneurs to understand that a business is a living, breathing entity. The brain and the heart — your strategic processes, and your marketing and branding — need to be in line with where you want to go with your company. That's why it is so important that you understand your end goal. You need to understand where your prospects are going to come into the sales funnel. You need to understand what pathways they're going to be using to get into your sales funnel, and ultimately, converting to clients.

The MarketAtomy concept is designed to visually show new entrepreneurs what needs to be in place to develop these processes and these pathways, to convert these prospects from leads, to prospects, and ultimately to customers.

Call to Action!

For details and a helpful assessment tool to help uncover your passion, go to www.marketatomy. com/bktools under *"Passion Check."*

CHAPTER FIVE

Realizing Your Dreams

YOUR DREAMS ARE ACHIEVABLE

Growing up, I had a very vivid imagination. I remember learning that China was completely on the opposite side of the world from where we are. I had it in my head that if I dug a hole deep enough in the backyard, I would eventually reach China. Imagine the surprise on my mother's face when she questioned me as to why I was digging such a big hole and I told her.

Did I mention that I was a very gullible child and adult?

Perhaps it is because I am quick to trust, sometimes to my detriment. I was labeled a daydreamer by one of my teachers. I was staring out the window constantly, just daydreaming, thinking about what I wanted to do with my life. As a teenager, I enjoyed singing, but my mother often reminded me that I was tone-deaf and advised me to give up on that dream. As an adult, I encountered numerous people throughout my career who told me my ideas about how to streamline processes were unachievable.

Where would I be today if I had let those naysayers stop me from trying to reach my dream?

Don't get me wrong; the negative impact that they imprinted on my psyche will still interrupt my forward momentum from time to time, but now I know how to handle that negative feedback.

Many people have labeled me with attention deficit disorder, or ADD.

When both of my children ended up with ADD or attention deficit/hyperactivity disorder (ADHD), I thought, "Well, maybe there's something to this."

But if having dreams and moving toward those dreams is part of the ADD or ADHD process, I'm all for it.

Your Dreams Will Not Be Handed to You

The first thing I learned many years ago was that my dreams were not going to materialize out of thin air. Yes, perhaps I was a daydreamer as a child. My dreams comprised my ideas of what I wanted out of life, what would make me happy.

There were times that I wanted to sing. I still do. Although I know now that I am not tone-deaf, I do know that the talent for singing is not in my genes. So I sing for the fun of it. My daughter, however, must have inherited a recessive singing gene, because she came out of the womb singing and has not stopped a day in her life. Her father and I used to complain because she was always singing — in the car, at home, everywhere — and we kept trying to stop her. But she wouldn't! She loves to sing, and she has beautiful voice. You can ask her to sing any one of the Disney tunes, and she will give you a commanding performance in the most beautiful voice imaginable. The funny thing is, her daughter is taking after her at age four. Perhaps the singing gene was not dominant in me. It still resonated enough to pass onto my daughter and granddaughter.

I also wanted to be a fashion designer at one point. I learned to sew very well, and I made all of my daughter's clothes until she got to an age of making her own decisions about what she wanted to wear, which encompassed the extent of my fashion design career.

I have always had a talent for art and writing. Ever since I was a little girl, this was my fate. As a result, I have learned to use my talents for good, and, sometimes, maybe not so much good.

I remember when I was fourteen, and my mother had made me very angry. I used that anger to build a papier-mâché statue of a girl kneeling with her head in her hands, crying. It was my way of getting my anger out. It actually came out pretty well.

It was close to Mother's Day, and I decided to give it to my mom with a little sign attached that said, "How can people be so heartless?" from the song written by MacDermot, Ragni, and Rado and recorded by Three Dog Night, "Easy to Be Hard."

My hope was that she would get the message of how much she had hurt me, but that wasn't the case. Needless to say, she still has that statue today, but got rid of the sign.

I've digressed a little, but the point is that although I had many dreams, my art and writing were the ones that allowed me to express myself the most. Understanding this, I set out to build my career around what I enjoyed the most. I began as a journalist early in my career, and eventually pulled in my art to compliment my writing, through graphic design. I was seeking that happy melding of art and writing that I enjoyed so much. It worked, for a while.

Be Willing to Work for Your Dreams

While my dreams revolved around doing what I was good at, I was also a realist, and knew that I needed to make a living from what I enjoyed doing. Growing up the oldest of seven children in a household where every penny mattered, and the difficult choices of what we were going to spend our money on, one of the lessons I also learned is the importance of hard work and taking pride in your craft.

My father was a block mason, and laid blocks all day long in the hot sun. I remember my father driving me around in his truck and pointing out the shoddy craftsmanship throughout town as we rode around. He would point out the details that demonstrated that the person laying the blocks did not take pride in his work. My father knew that he was good, and therefore, was paid handsomely for it. As an entrepreneur, you need to believe in your abilities, and not be afraid to own up to your mistakes and learn from them. As part of that ownership, you also need not to be afraid to charge the market rate for your services. If you have value over the competition, you need to compute that into the overall cost as well. There will be times when your abilities will be questioned, and you will feel the need to back down.

Growing up, there were so many times that my dreams were challenged. When I went to Brazil, I can't tell you how many colleagues and peers in the United States thought I was crazy and foolish for attempting such a large undertaking.

They would say things like, "Women are not respected in Brazil. You're just wasting your time," or, "You don't have what they need. They have companies from all over the world weighing down on them for a piece of the action."

What they underestimated was my resolve. I went initially just to create inroads, relationships, and find out what was needed. I did not go to sell at first. It was a fact-finding mission. I learned the culture, and even a little bit of the language. I met with civic leaders, entrepreneurs, government officials, and people off the street. I wanted to become entrenched in their joys, beliefs, pain points, and psyche before I made any further determinations.

As a result, I learned what drove them. I learned how to communicate, and ultimately, how to get them to seek out what I had to offer, and respect me for the businesswoman I was. What I also learned was that they are a lot like us: proud, enterprising, and stubborn in a lot of ways, but true friends in the end, with a healthy appetite for competition, which is why they are always trying to keep up with the new technological advances made in the United States. Hence, the major lessons I learned about Brazil is that they are great visionaries, but lack the ability to plan and strategize. They tend to jump in with both feet, and slide on the way down. Not always the best scenario, as experienced with my bus accident in 2012.

There Will Be Roadblocks

There will always be stumbling blocks along the way in business and in life.

If there weren't, how could we as human beings grow into strong, dynamic, well-rounded individuals?

Your roadblocks are what make your dreams, and you, stronger. By examining your roadblocks, you uncover what is at their source, and how you can break through them.

The dream of entrepreneurship is organic in nature. It evolves and grows as you do. It transforms and adjusts to the environment. The more you nurture it, the faster success comes, and the stronger you are to overcoming and breaking through those barriers that hold you back. By not feeding the dream, and sitting back waiting for something for happen, you lose that forward momentum, and the dream ultimately dies.

The MarketAtomy learning environment is all about nurturing. As entrepreneurs, knowledge is the key to success. Short of going back to school and gaining an MBA, the knowledge needed to grow comes in the form of lessons learned, either your own or others. It's called the School of Hard Knocks. Going back for an MBA is not only time-consuming, but it's often not set in the real world, generally. I'm not saying this is the case across the board, but an MBA teaches more theory than real-life lessons. As a business owner, sometimes you don't have the time to go back for an MBA and keep your business running at the same time. In addition, learning from the mistakes and successes of others are more substantial and fulfilling than those based on theory. Understanding this going in is half the battle. The other half is accepting that you don't know it all, and there are those eager to help you achieve your dreams.

The fact is that dreams are only achievable if you actually believe that they can be achievable. Therefore, you have to put some action behind it.

YOUR DREAMS ARE YOUR OWN

This is something that's really close to my heart and something that I strongly believe you need to evaluate moving forward as entrepreneurs, and why many people go into business in the first place.

First, your dreams are yours alone. They manifest from within your subconscious, your soul. They are your compass, your reason for being. They are driven by your desires; therefore, it's important to understand that they are unique to you. No one else can dictate the course you take in making them a reality.

No One Else Can Dictate Your Dreams

John Maxwell wrote a little book called, *Own Your Dreams*. I highly recommend it.

In it, he states, "A genuine dream is a picture and blueprint of a person's purpose and potential."

Or, as his friend Sharon Hull says, "A dream is the seed of possibility planted in the soul of a human being, which calls him to pursue a unique path to the realization of his purpose."

The resonating point that I got out of this book is that your dreams are a reflection of your life's purpose. Sadly, what happens many times is that your dreams are actually a manifestation of someone else's dreams — your parents, your spouse, your children — and not your own. Those of us who are parents know how easy it can be to try and steer children one way or another. Often it's not intentional, but in the overall dependent relationship that comes in the parent-child relationship, and the child wanting to please the parent, the choice is made.

There are many reasons people want to push their dreams onto someone else. Some may include the fear of change, or the fear of failure, or even the fear of having an unflattering light shed on them. In order to excel in business, the dream must be owned by the entrepreneur. The dream and the passion behind it are what drive the overall forward momentum for the business.

Keeping Up With the Joneses Isn't the Answer

Many times I've heard entrepreneurs say the main reason they went into business in the first place was for financial freedom; to be able to do or buy what they want when they want it. If that is the primary reason for going into business, I'm afraid you're just going to fail.

Ask any entrepreneur who is at the point of financial freedom—with the beautiful homes, the fancy cars, and the exotic trips—what their secret is, and they will all say the same things:

- Hard work
- Blood
- Sweat
- Tears
- A lot—a *lot*—of patience

That is why it is so important to own your dream. The purpose behind a dream keeps you in the game. Once that spark is gone, the business dies. There's nothing driving it anymore. You can get the money anywhere. Maybe not to the level you dreamed of, but the primary reason for going into business in the first place has to be something deeper than financial gain. Money comes as a result of the purpose behind the business.

My purpose behind MarketAtomy was to help first-stage companies succeed in a difficult entrepreneurial climate. I've had many professionals tell me that I'm setting myself up for failure, because first-stage businesses can't afford my services, which is why many of my competitors have taken the route of targeting second-stage businesses. Sure, second-stage businesses are established and can afford to pay for the services that my colleagues offer similar to mine.

The fact remains, however, that there are still more than five hundred thousand new businesses starting each year in the United States. Of those, more than 85 percent fail within the first two years of opening their doors.

Why?

Many quoted reasons include:

- Under-capitalization
- Poor leadership
- Poor pricing
- Poor financial management

The greatest reason is that the majority of them did not have the knowledge base to go into business in the first place. If they had the skills to birth and grow a business, they would have the expertise to work through all of the other reasons businesses fail. They had a great product or service, but no customers.

When more than 60 percent of the nation's gross domestic product (GDP) is made up of small businesses, how can we ignore those owners who are trying to live the American Dream but whose businesses have not reached the critical second stage yet?

I made a conscious decision to be that resource to these companies. I want to make a dent in the overall number of business failures of first-stage companies. I was tired of seeing friends, family, and colleagues mortgaging their homes and pillaging their 401Ks to open a business that they did not have the skill set to manage and grow.

Only You Can Validate Your Dreams

As stated before, my dream is my own, but I do agree with those who warned me that I have a very hard road ahead of me. I chose the market that, although it's not limited in size because there are a lot of them, it is limited in available dollars. With that in mind, I had to come up with an efficient means of providing the help these startups needed so desperately, without giving up too much of myself and my family. MarketAtomy is the validation of my dream.

My clarity came when talking to some friends about the increase in consulting and learning environments. I had already spent the previous two years working on the MarketAtomy concept and its delivery method, so I had a proven business model. I just had to figure out how to deliver it to the masses while building a content generator that was not reliant completely on my team members and me.

As I've said, MarketAtomy was developed a couple years ago around an effort to explain to my clients the many components that needed to be in place to succeed in business. This included more than just the marketing and branding side; it encompassed the financial, operations, the whole kit and caboodle.

I illustrated the concept around the human body to make it easy to understand, because entrepreneurship is organic, and there are many different moving parts that affect the whole dynamic. The MarketAtomy learning environment was developed around the original concept to respond to each of the different components and the educational aspects that accompany them. In other words, we took the MarketAtomy concept that had been proven over the previous two years to the next level. We created an online learning environment and thus opened up the market.

Because your dreams are your own, you need to be behind them 100 percent. You need to own them, because there are going to be naysayers out there. There are going to be people who are going to challenge you on your dream and on your approach to that dream. You need to own it completely in order to maintain the needed momentum.

KNOW WHERE YOU'RE GOING, SO YOU'LL KNOW WHEN YOU GET THERE

One topic that is most often addressed when consulting with a new client is the concept of an exit strategy. Many business owners do not understand this. The reason we emphasize the end at the very beginning is because, many times, new entrepreneurs go into business without any idea of where they want to take their business.

The point being, if you don't know where you're going, how are you going to know if you've arrived?

If you don't know the milestone markers along the way, how are you going to be able to measure whether you're moving forward or are just stagnant?

Ultimately, the details are often found in the unknown. Until you know, you can't iron out the details to get there.

You Must Have a Strategy

Imagine you're planning a trip to a city in a distant country, let's say Timbuktu. It's not as though you can just jump on a plane to Timbuktu and expect everything to magically fall into place. You have to first understand what needs to be done to enter the country, such as a passport, visa, or immunizations. Speaking of immunizations, you need to know whether the area has any health issues you need to be aware of, like contaminated water or high crime areas. God forbid a coup were to happen while you're there; knowing the political climate going in is important.

With the preliminaries out of the way, you need to outline and plan your trip:

- Lodging
- Transportation in country
- Managing the language

You wouldn't consider going into a foreign country — or anywhere for that matter — without a plan of action to get there.

So why would you consider starting a business without a plan in place?

Until now, you've probably been someone's employee and only had to worry about the responsibilities of your particular position. You managed the expectations because you knew your job and your capabilities. You were in your own little piece of Corporate America, and you more than likely had a boss looking over your shoulder to make sure you remained on track.

Now, as a business owner, there is so much to manage and know, that you're probably feeling overwhelmed and drowning in a sea of doubt. You don't have anyone holding you accountable to your promises to your customers, to your employees, or even yourself. You're overwhelmed and worried, not only about how to find the customers you need to keep the doors open, but how to ensure they get what they pay for, and remain happy with your services.

You feel as though you are the only one capable of ensuring this happens, so you wear that hat. Then, you worry daily about the finances. After all, that is why you went into business in the first place. You worry about the cash flow, making sure there is enough money coming in to cover the money going out. Because this is a critical part of the business, you don't trust anyone else to manage it, so you put on your other hat and you handle it, and so on.

Before you know it, you are working so much in the business that you don't have time to take care of the customers you have, let alone the ones you need to bring in to keep the sales funnel primed. It's important to reevaluate and strategize, before you are forced to close the doors, either because you are losing customers left and right, or the cash flow is not there to keep the doors open, or both for that matter. Running a business by the seat of your pants is a dangerous way to operate. Before you know it, it will be completely out of your control.

You Must Know Your Exit Strategy

This is one of those chicken-or-egg scenarios. Sometimes I struggle whether I introduce the endgame or the exit strategy, or the one that we just talked about, having a strategy in general. In order to put the strategy together, you have to know what the exit plan is. As indicated earlier, knowing the endgame is imperative to understanding and mapping out the process for reaching it.

What is the ultimate goal for your company?

Is it to franchise?

Is it to pass onto your children?

Perhaps it's to build up to a certain level, and then to sell it.

What is the ultimate endgame you should be working for, or you're working so hard for?

For that matter, how are you going to protect yourself to ensure that you are able to enjoy the celebration at the end?

What a lot of entrepreneurs do not realize is the importance of Key Man insurance to protect yourself and your key leadership. Should something happen to you or a key player in your business, you don't want those shares of your company going to somebody who does not have the same goal or motivation in the company.

Have you considered how you're going to ensure that your employees remain with you, and don't take your best secrets or intellectual property to your competitor?

All of these are questions that should be asked early on in your entrepreneurial endeavors.

Take Action

The only thing that keeps a business growing is momentum. That momentum is the direct result of your purpose behind your dream and taking action, and not just action, but proactive measures. It's the reason for strategic planning.

One of the biggest mistakes that small business owners make is to forget all about the planning once the business is open. All the work that went into the strategy ends up being put on the shelf, in lieu of working in your business. As a result, all forward momentum halts, because the only action being taken is reactive. Reactive action is time-consuming and exhausting, and it produces very little.

Proactive action creates momentum, which in itself creates more opportunities for growth. It takes on a life of its own and becomes organic. Managing proactive actions is much easier, because it can be controlled through strategic planning, whereas reactive action is controlled by external forces, often leaving very little time for planning a different course of action. It's the difference between validating your business idea and creating the perfect logo, or examining your motivation for creating a new business this week, or perhaps shutting down from overload, to pinpointing the source and breaking through that overload. It's all about taking action.

To take action, you need to know what you're working for, and why you're working for it. If your dream has a purpose behind it, you have a strategy behind that purpose, and know how you're going to get to your endgame, then your business is a success.

Call to Action!

If you are ready to get started on your own Marketing Strategy, check out our Marketing Strategy Approach template at www.marketatomy. com/bktools. Why wait? Take that first step now!

Conclusion

I originally came up with the MarketAtomy concept because I was so frustrated at seeing so many friends and colleagues wasting a whole bunch of money starting a business they really had no business running. They just did not know what they were doing. I wanted to figure out how I could help them gain the knowledge that they needed to keep their businesses running and growing, so ultimately their dream would be successful. Nearly three years after introducing the MarketAtomy Concept, I have uncovered a whole family needing guidance from a business-birthing coach. People who have *been there, done that* and who are eager to help.

The main thing I discovered with entrepreneurs was that they all went into business because they had a product or service that they did well or knew well. They felt that they could make money at it, but ultimately they had no understanding of how to run a business, how to price their product or service, or how to attract customers. I explained to them that without customers, you can have the best product or service in the world, but there is no business. I told them it's like being pregnant without a way to deliver, which is where I came up with the name of the book, *MarketAtomy: What to Expect When Expecting a Business.*

Just like going through the birth of a child, you go through the birth of a business. You have the gestation period, which is the dream period. You decide you want to go into business. Then you move into the birth of the business. This is where the hard work starts, and if you don't have the appropriate knowledge base, it's even more difficult. Finally, once you start the business, you have to grow that business. Just like an infant grows through the elementary school years, into the teen years, and into adulthood, you want to grow a business so it moves through the infancy stage on into maturity. Ultimately, you can retire from the business, and reach whatever goal you have.

The MarketAtomy concept was developed to show new business owners what needs to be in place to birth your business and grow it. It's all based around the human body. The heart of your business is marketing and branding. That marketing and branding message is what drives everything else in the business, from the tools that you use to get the message out into the marketplace, to the services that you provide to your customers in order to keep them coming back, to the pricing strategies you implement for your product or service. These are all things that new entrepreneurs, new business owners, need to understand before going into business.

I started to implement this process with my clients to teach them what they needed. What I realized very quickly, early on, is there's only one of me. There were so many new business owners who needed my help, and I had to determine how I was going to establish a business model that allowed me to reach the masses without having to put myself in front of them every time. That is why I introduced the MarketAtomy learning platform, which has been set up to help small business owners gain the knowledge base that they need in their own time frames, in their own homes, through their own processes. And if they need additional help, they can reach out.

I will tell you that I have gotten a lot of flak because I am reaching out to first-stage companies. As we all know, first-stage companies are those that are struggling. It's like when you're first married, or you're first out on your own, and you struggle to pay rent and utilities and everything else. You're doing the same with a business, and therefore cash flow is limited.

What it all boils down to is those statistics mentioned earlier: more than five hundred thousand small businesses start every year in the United States. Eighty-five percent of those, on average, fail within the first two years. To me, there's no reason for that if they have the needed education available to them.

But unfortunately, most organizations set up to help small businesses are only there to help at the second stage. Many of these new start-ups never make it to the end-stage. Very few agencies are available to provide assistance to small businesses at the first stage, when they're first starting out. My goal with MarketAtomy is to make a dent in the number of small businesses that are failing in the United States, by providing a platform to offer the education needed to build and grow their businesses without having to go back to school for an MBA. I cannot do this alone, which is why I have enlisted the help of many friends and experts across the nation to help in this endeavor.

Many of these small businesses are already active and they're losing money. What we're trying to do is stop the financial bleed. We're trying to give them the tools that they need to turn their company around through the MarketAtomy learning concept. That is my heart and the whole reason behind MarketAtomy.

Check out www.marketatomy.com/nextsteps to continue your entrepreneurial journey.

Next Steps

I'm currently working on a sequel to *MarketAtomy: What to Expect When Expecting a Business*, called *MarketAtomy: Full Body Scan*.. In this sequel we will be breaking down each of the components of the MarketAtomy Concept. This will be a coauthored book in conjunction with a dear friend and new entrepreneur who will be going through the entire MarketAtomy Concept, highlighting her experience.

Additionally, I invite you to visit the MarketAtomy Learning Platform at www.MarketAtomy.com, to launch in the second half of 2017. It is my hope that the stories revealed in *MarketAtomy: Full Body Scan* will resonate and provide additional lessons learned to help you grow your business. Check out www.marketatomy.com/nextsteps to continue your entrepreneurial journey.

About the Author

Danna is a business growth strategist and CEO of MarketAtomy, LLC. Her passion is working with small and start-up entrepreneurs to ensure that they start out on the right foot and stay on the path to financial freedom. As an experienced business coach and strategist, Danna understands the intricacies involved in starting and running a successful business. Her efforts extend beyond the initial strategic planning process to the implementation and monitoring phase. As an intricate component in her clients' business structure, she works diligently to keep her clients accountable and on track to fulfilling their success goals.

MarketAtomy's online learning environment, due to beta launch late 2017, is an environment where early-stage entrepreneurs can receive the education and guidance needed to successfully build an infrastructure on which to grow their business. It can be found at www.MarketAtomy.com.

A graduate of the University of Central Florida's College of Business, Danna holds degrees in both marketing and management information systems (MIS). She brings more than thirty-five years of strategic planning experience in business, marketing, and business development, both nationally and internationally.

Danna is not only a professional business growth strategist, but also an international strategist in Brazil, a public speaker, and number-one bestselling author on Amazon with her first book, *Success from the Heart*.

www.ingramcontent.com/pod-product-compliance
Lightning Source LLC
Chambersburg PA
CBHW071154200326
41519CB00018B/5226